*God's Wisdom for
Making Peace*

God's Wisdom for Making Peace

Daily Devotions in the Letter to Philemon

Paul S. Jeon

RESOURCE *Publications* · Eugene, Oregon

GOD'S WISDOM FOR MAKING PEACE
Daily Devotions in the Letter to Philemon

Copyright © 2018 Paul S. Jeon. All rights reserved. Except for brief quotations in critical publications or reviews, no part of this book may be reproduced in any manner without prior written permission from the publisher. Write: Permissions, Wipf and Stock Publishers, 199 W. 8th Ave., Suite 3, Eugene, OR 97401.

Resource Publications
An Imprint of Wipf and Stock Publishers
199 W. 8th Ave., Suite 3
Eugene, OR 97401

www.wipfandstock.com

PAPERBACK ISBN: 978-1-5326-5650-7
HARDCOVER ISBN: 978-1-5326-5651-4
EBOOK ISBN: 978-1-5326-5652-1

Manufactured in the U.S.A.   OCTOBER 19, 2018

To Luke & Rebecca

Contents

Acknowledgments | *ix*
Series Introduction | *xi*
Brief Background on the Letter to Philemon | *xv*
Day 1: Philemon 1a | 1
Day 2: Philemon 1b–2 | 3
Day 3: Philemon 3 | 5
Day 4: Philemon 4 | 7
Day 5: Philemon 5 | 9
Day 6: Philemon 6a | 11
Day 7: Philemon 6b | 13
Day 8: Philemon 6c | 15
Day 9: Philemon 7 | 17
Day 10: Philemon 8–9 | 19
Day 11: Philemon 8–9 | 21
Day 12: Philemon 10a | 23
Day 13: Philemon 10b–11 | 25
Day 14: Philemon 12 | 27
Day 15: Philemon 13–14a | 29
Day 16: Philemon 14b | 31
Day 17: Philemon 15 | 33

Day 18: Philemon 16 | 35
Day 19: Philemon 17 | 37
Day 20: Philemon 18 | 39
Day 21: Philemon 19 | 41
Day 22: Philemon 20 | 43
Day 23: Philemon 21 | 45
Day 24: Philemon 22 | 47
Day 25: Philemon 23–24 | 49
Day 26: Philemon 24 | 51
Day 27: Philemon 25 | 53
   Summary | 55
   Bibliography | 61

Acknowledgments

FIRST, I THANK BRIAN Forman. As with every endeavor I undertake, this project came to fruition only through his steadfast partnership. Second, I thank the Gibson family, who generously provided an opportunity for me to get away to focus on the final manuscript for this devotional. Third, I thank Karis Oh, who in passing suggested the idea for this book. Finally, I thank my wife, who is my rock.

Series Introduction

This short book on the Letter to Philemon is the first installment in this devotional series. The idea for this series came from Karis, a member at my church who expressed her preference to delve into specific sections of the Bible. While committed to reading the Bible cover to cover as often as possible, she was at a point in life where she wanted to go beyond "passive" reading. In short, she wanted to engage in reading that entailed pausing, reflecting, and praying over shorter units. This series is my attempt to meet this desire.

Three preliminary remarks to the series might enhance your experience of this devotional.

First, before penning anything, I memorized the letter (which is only a single chapter comprised of twenty-five verses). Bible memorization is a regular practice of mine first encouraged by my mother during the summer between third and fourth grade and later reiterated by my professor in New Testament during seminary. It's far easier for me to comment on any part of the Bible when it's in me (literally). Thus, I spent a month memorizing the letter and jotting down random thoughts on my iPhone as they came throughout the day. Only after feeling like "it's in me" did I begin concrete work on this devotional.

I encourage you to memorize as much of the letter as possible, before and while working through this devotional. Life is complicated, and often we lack crystal-clear answers to any given situation. This is where "biblical instincts" come in, instincts borne out of years of Bible memorization, meditation, and application. The common response is, "I can't memorize chunks of the Bible—my memory has gotten so bad." My encouragement: "You'll be amazed at what you can do once you get started." But it will require much deliberation—taking pockets of time throughout the day to set aside social media and let your mind sit on a verse or two. Few things have served my soul better than Bible memorization.

Second, I have no interest in saying anything innovative. My assumption is that when people pick up a devotional, they are looking to hear an amplification of what God says in his revealed Word. Thus, my burden with each entry has been to bring out both the meaning and the intended effect of the text. To this end, I made an analytical outline of the letter using the original Greek and referenced the best commentaries to ensure I was coming as close to the original meaning and rhetorical purpose of the apostle Paul.[1] Nevertheless, the final output was purposefully nonacademic: I tried to use plain language to minimize distraction and to amplify the meaning of the inspired text.

Finally, each installment in this series focuses on a single topic. To be sure, we touch on sub-topics related to the main subject, but, all in all, I focus on a single topic. The reason for this is because of my growing belief that we accomplish far more in life by trying to do far less.[2] Personal change is hard. I'll never become more generous, less angry, more integrous, less covetous by tackling everything at once. Instead, focusing on one virtue for at least six to twelve months leads to deeper and lasting change. If the reader detects some redundancy as a result of this approach, I will have done my job.

This devotional focuses on the topic of reconciliation. Closely related are the topics of mediation and winsome communication. As I have written elsewhere, reconciliation is a lost mandate that needs to be recovered in the Church today.[3] In my experience (admittedly limited), many sincere Christians seem fine with allowing

---

1. Noteworthy are the commentaries of Peter O'Brien, N. T. Wright, Douglas Moo, and Dick Lucas. Also, in this commentary I use the *English Standard Version* translation except in a few instances.

2. See Charles Duhigg's *The Power of Habit* and Gary Keller's *The One Thing*, which suggest the same.

3. See my comments in *Unreconciled*.

unreconciled relationships to persist—as if reconciliation were not a priority in the eyes of God! Similarly, for a variety of sociological reasons we will not get into here, Christians have taken a passive stance in facilitating peace between unreconciled believers in their own churches. As we'll see in this letter, peace between Onesimus and Philemon would not have been possible had Paul not "brokered a deal." Finally, for some, "speaking the truth in love" (Ephesians 4:15) has become license for straightforward and harsh speech. Yet as the apostle models here, mediation between unreconciled parties is a messy affair and therefore requires the use of judicious language and disarming engagement.[4] For all these reasons, the Letter to Philemon stands as a model of how we can mature as makers of peace in our churches. My hope is that this extended reflection on the letter will facilitate that goal.

> "Let the word of Christ dwell in you richly . . ."
> —Colossians 3:16

---

4. Wright, *Epistles*, 164: "[The Letter to Philemon] is no mere casual note, but a carefully crafted and sensitively worded piece, employing tact and irony."

Brief Background on the Letter to Philemon[1]

HISTORICAL RECONSTRUCTION IS ALWAYS a bit tricky. I can hardly remember what I did last Wednesday. How much more challenging must it be to piece together a detailed and accurate background of exactly what took place many years ago.

Still, the letter itself does provide some basic clues. First, the main cast of characters. There is Paul who is writing from prison. Then there is Philemon, a leader among the church that meets in his house; we can assume Philemon was a man of means. Finally, there's Onesimus, apparently a runaway slave who came to faith through Paul's ministry and has now been sent back to his master, Philemon. An important detail in all this is that both Philemon and Onesimus have come to faith (at separate times) through Paul.

What's a bit murky are the details of the conflict between Philemon and Onesimus. That Onesimus abandoned his master suggests that the conflict was bad enough that the two had to be divinely separated. At a first glance (and this might very well be the case), it appears that Onesimus had wronged Philemon. Badly. But toward the end of the letter, Paul indicates through the suggestive statement, "*If* he has wronged you," that this might not have been the case and that Philemon is essentially overreacting. Whatever the conflict actually entails, we know that Philemon is nowhere near a point of wanting to be reconciled with Onesimus

---

1. Much more detailed and scholarly background information can be found in the Introduction sections of the commentaries previously mentioned.

even though both now share a common faith and fellowship in the Lord.

Paul, wanting to see the two reconciled and concerned for how a continued unreconciled state will impact the general community of faith, pens this letter to encourage Philemon to receive back Onesimus. Paul is fully aware of how tense the situation is. Therefore, rather than adopting a direct approach, he opts for a winsome and indirect appeal by identifying himself with both persons and then highlighting their new relationship to each other through Paul and in Christ.[2] For this reason, the Letter to Philemon should be understood not just as a call to make peace but also as a model for winsome mediation. Indeed, "no part of the New Testament more clearly demonstrates integrated Christian thinking and living. It offers a blend, utterly characteristic of Paul, of love, wisdom, humour, gentleness, tact, and above all Christian and human maturity."[3]

---

2. Wright, *Epistles*, 168: "As Luther saw, Paul plays Christ in the drama, identifying himself with both sinner and offended party, so making peace . . ."

3. Ibid, 170.

Day 1

Philemon 1a

"Paul, a prisoner for Christ Jesus"

NOTABLE IS PAUL'S USE of the identifier "prisoner" instead of his more typical title "apostle." The latter conveys authority, the former weakness. Why does Paul do this? After all, it's human tendency to highlight one's status. Reflecting on this question is important because it provides some insight into the content, purpose, and strategy of the letter.

In this letter, Paul pleads on behalf of Onesimus, a nobody. In stark contrast, Philemon is a man of means. Not only that, he is a man of spiritual stature: Paul recognizes him as a "beloved fellow worker" (v. 1b) and as a wonderful host (the church meets in his house; v. 2). So why does Paul refer to himself as a lowly prisoner? He does so to identify with the weak and ostracized—in this case, Onesimus. This, after all, is what Christ did for sinners by becoming a man and dying on the cross. And this is what we are called to do—to plead for the weak and powerless in large part by identifying with them.

By lowering himself to identify with Onesimus, Paul hopes to move his friend and coworker Philemon toward compassion and "gospel-sobriety." Perhaps by recalling Paul's chains, Philemon will be more inclined to meet the apostle's request (which he states later in the letter). Philemon himself might even be moved to surrender his rights in order to forgive and embrace Onesimus.

Prayer

Lord Jesus, thank you for becoming nothing in order to make me something. Thank you for becoming a prisoner so that I might become free from sin and death. Help me now to lift my eyes and consider the weak and disenfranchised. Give me grace through your Spirit to align myself with people like Onesimus. Finally, bless those who are suffering even now in order to draw others to you. Amen.

Day 2

Philemon 1b–2

"and Timothy our brother, To Philemon our beloved fellow worker and Apphia our sister and Archippus our fellow soldier, and the church in your house"

Notice the use of family and fellowship language in the opening greeting. Timothy and Apphia are respectively identified as "brother" and "sister." Philemon is a "fellow worker" and Archippus a "fellow soldier." Moreover, the believers meet in Philemon's "house." Paul could not make clearer the communal nature of the Christian life: life in Christ is—to borrow the title of Bonhoeffer's book—life together.

Though Philemon is the primary recipient of this letter, the entire church, as the greeting suggests, would have heard the letter as it was read aloud in the presence of all. This point is important to highlight. Not only would the public reading of the letter have placed some pressure on Philemon to heed Paul's exhortation about receiving Onesimus as a brother in Christ (v. 17). It would have also been a reminder to all the believers that there is really no such thing as a private conflict: whatever affects a few will inevitably affect all within God's family. This isn't to suggest that we must make public every small conflict. But this is to expose the fallacy in supposing that our individual conflicts won't have any bearing on the fellowship of the saints.

Unreconciled relationships hurt the family of God. Sometimes the impact is immediate and obvious. Other times the impact is subtler but no less damaging. For instance, a refusal to be reconciled can slowly lead to a toxic culture where unreconciled relationships represent the cultural norm. Recognizing that this is not the way things are supposed to be in God's house, Paul highlights from the outset the familial nature of Christian fellowship: we are brothers and sisters and fellow workers and soldiers in Christ.

Prayer

Father in heaven, I confess that my view of the Christian life is far too individualistic. I confess that I have not appreciated the reality of being adopted into your family through Christ. And this is perhaps nowhere more evident than in my naïve perspective on "personal" conflict. I have failed to consider how my refusal to pursue reconciliation has stumbled my brothers and sisters. Help me now to be more thoughtful about how my words and actions affect the family of God. Amen.

Day 3

Philemon 3

"Grace to you and peace from God our Father and
the Lord Jesus Christ"

Paul's letter begins with this prayer of blessing: "Grace to you and peace . . ." The frequency of this prayer, however, should not desensitize us to its significance. "Grace" refers to the unmerited favor God has shown us in Christ Jesus. It also has the sense of "empowering grace"—that which enables obedience. "Peace" refers to our new reconciled state with God through Jesus Christ. Previously, because of sin, we were enemies of God; now we are counted as friends and family. The location of this prayer at the beginning of the letter reminds Philemon and the believers that meet in his house that above anything else they are recipients of grace and reconciliation. Irrespective of the demands of the moment, from the perspective of eternity they are objects of mercy and favor.

The apostle identifies the source of such grace and peace as "our Father and the Lord Jesus Christ." The implication is that, on his own accord, God decided to show sinners kindness and pursue reconciliation. That God was the "first-mover" is important to highlight and remember. In this letter, Paul summons Philemon to extend grace and pursue peace with Onesimus. But before making such a summons, he wants Philemon to remember the grace and peace he has first received "from God our Father and the Lord Jesus Christ." This, after all, is the nature of the Christian life—to forgive because we have been forgiven, to love because we have been loved, to give because we have received so much more than we could ever ask or imagine.

Prayer

God, thank you for taking the initiative to show me kindness when I deserved wrath, for making peace when I rejected your rule over my life. Thank you for sending your Son, the Lord Jesus Christ, to show me in a tangible way how much you love me and the extent you were willing to go to restore our relationship. All this I recognize is according to your mercy, not my achievements. Help me now to extend to others the grace and peace I have received from you. By doing so, may I glorify you. Amen.

Day 4

Philemon 4

"I thank my God always when I remember you in my prayers"

PAUL BEGINS THE BODY of his letter by sharing his regular remembrance of Philemon in prayer. Douglas Moo comments: "'Remembering' people in prayer . . . involves not only the mental activity of considering them and their needs but also calling on *God* to consider them and act for their benefit."[1] Paul knows that the work of reconciliation is difficult. In fact, it's almost impossible unless God steps into a situation and stirs the hearts of his people to remember the grace they have received and been called to give. In conflict, whether it involves us directly or indirectly, we must appreciate the critical role that prayer plays in bringing about reconciliation.

We may wonder, "Why is prayer necessary? Doesn't God want to see people reconciled? Why must we call on God to act on their behalf?" Few have given a better explanation as to why prayer is necessary than Augustine: "Pray as though everything depends on God, and work as though everything depended on you."[2] Indeed, as Calvin centuries later said: "As for Himself, what He has determined to give, of His own free will and even before He is asked, He promises to give all the same, in response to our prayers.

---

1. Moo, *Letters*, 386 (italics mine).
2. Quoted in Wiersbe, who goes on to say: "It is when God's people get out of balance and overemphasize either sovereignty or responsibility that the church loses power" (*Bible Exposition*, 419).

Keep hold of both points, then: our prayers are anticipated by Him in His freedom, yet, what we ask we gain by prayer."[3]

Prayer

Lord, teach me to pray about all things but especially about reconciliation. There are conflicts in my life that will not be resolved unless you move your people to remember and fulfill their calling to be peacemakers. Forgive me for neglecting prayer. I acknowledge that "many things will be achieved by prayer and that many things will not be achieved without prayer."[4] Therefore, I commit anew to praying for reconciliation among those in broken relationships. Amen.

---

3. Calvin, *Calvin's New Testament Commentaries*, 204.
4. Frame, *Systematic Theology*, 1054.

Day 5

Philemon 5

"because I hear of your love and of the faith that you have toward the Lord Jesus and for all the saints"

VERSE 5 DETAILS WHY Paul gives thanks to God for Philemon. The verse follows a chiastic structure:

A: your love
  B: your faith
  B': toward the Lord Jesus Christ
A': for all the saints

Paul is thankful for Philemon's faith toward the Lord Jesus Christ (B-B'), which is "proven" by his love for the saints (A-A'). Here we are reminded of the unbreakable tie between our relationship with God and our relationship with other Christians, the people of God. The apostle John explains: "If anyone says, 'I love God,' and hates his brother, he is a liar; for he who does not love his brother whom he has seen cannot love God whom he has not seen" (1 John 4:20). In conflict, many believers tend to forget this basic truth. Faith in Jesus and love for the saints, expressed especially in making peace, are inseparable.

Paul includes an important detail. He is thankful for Philemon's love "for *all* the saints." Thus far, Philemon has shown a commitment to embrace all believers irrespective of their gender, class, and ethnicity. This accords with the gospel that "has been made known to *all* nations, according to the command of the eternal God" (Romans 16:26). God's will is for us to pursue and enjoy new relationships in Christ Jesus that are marked by intimate diversity. Indeed, a mark of true conversion is a profound change in the makeup of our day-to-day relationships.

Prayer

Father, I have convinced myself into believing that I can have a personal relationship with you while keeping a safe distance from other Christians. I confess that I limit my friendships only to individuals who are most similar to me. Most of all, I confess that I have allowed certain broken relationships to persist for far too long, supposing in these "special cases" that faith in Jesus and love for the saints can be separated. Forgive me for such folly. Help me to discern those whom I must love better as an expression of my faith in your Son. Amen.

Day 6

Philemon 6a

"and I pray that the sharing of your faith"

Verse 6 summarizes both the content of Paul's prayer on behalf of Philemon and the message of the letter. As such, we will dedicate the next several devotions to meditating on its significance.

What does Paul mean by "the sharing of your faith"? Perhaps the best place to start is the term "faith." What happens when you put your faith in Jesus for salvation (or what should happen)? In Acts 9:18–19, we're told that after regaining his sight, the apostle Paul was baptized and then joined the disciples at Damascus. This is important to highlight. Paul did not immediately preach the gospel nor did he go into isolation to spend one-on-one time with the Lord. Instead, he joined in fellowship with other believers. As we noted in the last devotion, faith in the Lord Jesus Christ always involves identification with the people Christ has saved.

When we place our faith in Jesus for salvation, God justifies us *and* adopts us into his family. This is what Paul means by "the sharing of your faith," which could be translated as "fellowship produced by faith." Because this fellowship flows from a mutual faith in Christ, it is unique. It is unlike any membership we might have elsewhere. This new fellowship in Christ involves a deep identification with its members akin to the intimate bond we share with our family. Moreover, with it come both benefits and responsibilities that we experience uniquely and wonderfully, again, in the context of family. Paul's prayer and the burden throughout this letter is that Philemon would come to see himself and his situation—indeed, all of life—through the perspective of belonging to this fellowship.

Prayer

Lord Jesus, you taught your disciples to pray, "Our Father who art in heaven." The identification of God as "Father" helps me to see that your salvation entails being adopted into the family of God. Also, that I am to pray "Our Father" reminds me that your family includes the many you have redeemed by your blood. As I continue to meditate on this letter, deepen my conviction that I belong to your family and teach me to adopt new patterns of life that accord with this new reality. Amen.

Day 7

Philemon 6b

"may become effective for the full knowledge of every good thing that is in us"

"Lord, what is your will for my life? What good work are you calling me to?" These are important questions for us to ask. After all, we regularly pray, "Your kingdom come, your will be done, on earth as it is in heaven" (Matthew 6:10). It's fitting for us to ask, then, what "good thing" we can do to materialize this prayer in our individual lives?

The second half of verse 6 gives guidance for discerning answers to such questions. To the surprise and perhaps even chagrin of some, the Bible doesn't call us to retreat into isolation (though personal retreats can be helpful). The Bible doesn't call us to fast and pray for supernatural revelation (though we should regularly pray and fast). Instead, the apostle Paul says that we should engage in deep fellowship with other believers. By doing so, we will come to a deep and practical understanding—"full knowledge"—of every good work that God is calling us to as we better understand every good work God is doing in and through the fellowship of believers. The somewhat ambiguous phrase "in us" can mean that there is good work God wants us to do with other believers or for other believers (or both). Either way, what's clear is that answers to how we are to steward our lives will be revealed only if we live in intimate fellowship with other believers. As an aside, this is why church membership is biblical and necessary for every follower of Christ.

Prayer

God, thank you for working in my heart a desire to live for you. As I grow in the gospel, I want to know how I can best steward my life to advance your kingdom. Thank you for providing a clear and concrete means of grace through your church. As I make every effort to serve faithfully as a member, make increasingly clear "every good thing" you are calling me to do with other believers and for other believers. Amen.

Day 8

Philemon 6c

"for the sake of Christ"

"So, whether you eat or drink, or whatever you do, do all to the glory of God" (1 Corinthians 10:31). The purpose of all of life is to honor God in anything and everything. Paul reiterates this by concluding verse 6 to Philemon with the words "for the sake of Christ." The motivation behind "every good thing" (v. 6b) that God has called us to do is not to advance our name and fame. It's not even to achieve a sense of personal satisfaction. Rather, all that we do should be "for the sake of Christ," to make his name known and honored among all nations. We can never be reminded of this too much.

All this sounds wonderful, and in many areas of life we do seek to uphold this command. When Christian couples speak about their family, they often say, "We want our family to be Christ-centered." Similarly, followers of Christ will at least ask and wonder, "How can I glorify God through my work?" For some reason, however, this principle (if we can call it that) is often dropped in conflicts. We don't ask, "How can I handle this situation in a way that honors Christ?" Instead, we fall back into the ways we've seen conflict addressed throughout our upbringings, or we follow our feelings and personalities. We engage in flight or fight, but we don't wrestle with the question of how to honor Christ in and throughout the conflict.

As we'll see in the next verse, Paul expresses his gratitude for the many ways Philemon has built up other believers. Already, he's recognized Philemon's generosity in letting the church meet at his home (v. 2). But now he is gently reminding Philemon to handle his personal conflict with Onesimus "for the sake of Christ." "Whatever you do, do all to the glory of God!"

Prayer

God, I confess that too often I live for myself instead of Christ. This is especially true when it comes to personal conflicts. I make decisions on the basis of convenience and personality. But I better understand now that conflicts offer unique opportunities to glorify you. Teach me to be more deliberate about my words and actions in times of conflict. Grant me wisdom to know how to honor Christ during these trying times. Amen.

Day 9

Philemon 7

"For I have derived much joy and comfort from your love, my brother, because the hearts of the saints have been refreshed through you"

VERSE 7 HIGHLIGHTS BOTH Philemon's profound impact on the believers that meet in his house and the tremendous responsibility he bears in the foreseeable future. Paul says that "the hearts of the saints have been refreshed through you." In the Bible, the "heart" refers to the "inner seat" of all our emotions, intellect, and affections. It captures our essence: it is the why behind everything we do. Paul says that Philemon's personal ministry has "refreshed" the hearts of believers, that is, his ministry has refreshed and renewed the saints in the deepest way possible. Recall the last time you had a good night's sleep and woke up feeling revived and ready for the day. This is the sort of long-term impact that Philemon's ministry had on the members of his church.[1]

But it is for this very reason that Philemon's conflict with Onesimus is so significant. As we'll see, the apostle is about to encourage reconciliation between the two. The letter wouldn't have been written had Philemon been willing to receive Onesimus on his own accord. There is little (if any) desire on the part of Philemon

---

1. Wright, *Epistles*, 178: "The verb here is in origin a military metaphor, signifying the rest that an army takes while on the march. The Colossian Christians, weary in their daily battles for the Lord, find in Philemon the refreshment and rest needed to renewed warfare."

for a restored relationship. Paul, however, knows how consequential this decision will be. In short, it will contribute to creating a culture where unreconciled relationships become the new norm. Some believers may become so stumbled by Philemon's refusal to extend grace and forgive (though he himself has received grace and been forgiven by God) that they become disengaged or even leave the church that meets in his house. Some might be tempted to follow his bad example. By highlighting the profound impact Philemon has had already, Paul is subtly reminding him that his conflict with Onesimus is not a private affair. Philemon's decision will affect the overall spiritual well-being of all the believers in his house.[2] What we do or don't do has ripple effects on all.

Prayer

Father in heaven, thank you for this reminder that my life matters. Each day my words and actions are either refreshing the hearts of believers or causing them to stumble. I pray again for your help with remembering that I belong to your family. Cause me to become all the more deliberate, especially during conflicts, to ask whether I am contributing to a culture of peacemaking or peace-breaking. Thank you for all the believers that have refreshed my heart over the years. Move me to do the same for others for your glory. Amen.

---

2. Ibid.: "The phrase 'my brother' [v. 7] . . . suggests that Paul sees in this ministry of Philemon something attractive and compelling . . ."

Day 10

Philemon 8–9

"Accordingly, though I am bold enough in Christ to command you to do what is required, yet for love's sake I prefer to appeal to you— I, Paul, an old man and now a prisoner also for Christ Jesus"

VERSE 8 BEGINS THE body of the letter. Here we discover why Paul has written this letter, namely to make an "appeal" to Philemon on behalf of Onesimus to welcome the latter. What is striking and noteworthy about his appeal is the manner in which he makes it. In this sense, the Letter to Philemon teaches us just as much about winsome persuasion as it does about reconciliation.

Paul's general approach to ministry was to model the very things he commanded. In these two verses he models humility and self-forgetfulness. First, Paul states that he is "bold enough in Christ to command you to do what is required." What he means is that because he is an apostle, he could simply tell Philemon what to do and avoid the hassle of mediation. Yet, he surrenders his rights—not unlike Christ—and opts to reason with Philemon. Paul does so because he knows that any reconciliation between Philemon and Onesimus will require Philemon to surrender what is supposedly owed to him (v. 18).

Second, Paul models not just humility but also self-forgetfulness. Notice the irony. He is "a prisoner" (v. 9) but he speaks nothing of his own freedom. Rather, his preoccupation is winning Onesimus's freedom. As an "old man," it would have been more convenient for him to spend his final days in quietness, altogether disconnected from the difficult work of reconciliation. Yet, setting aside his own preferences, he works for the good of both Philemon and Onesimus. This self-forgetfulness is an essential ingredient for reconciliation. In many instances, we must learn to set aside our grievances for the sake of the other person and for the sake of the wider community.

Prayer

Lord Jesus, I praise you for modeling humility and self-forgetfulness. Though in very nature God, you surrendered your rights by becoming a human being and dying on the cross in my place. You elevated the needs and preferences of others above your own. Through such humility and self-forgetfulness, you reconciled God and humanity. As I reflect on unreconciled relationships in my life, show me how to work out these qualities of humility and self-forgetfulness in specific and concrete ways in order to facilitate reconciliation. Amen.

Day 11

Philemon 8–9

"Accordingly, though I am bold enough in Christ to command you to do what is required, yet for love's sake I prefer to appeal to you— I, Paul, an old man and now a prisoner also for Christ Jesus"

WE REFLECT AGAIN ON these verses because there are two complementary points we must recognize. On the one hand, Paul uses the phrase "to do what is required" (v. 8). Throughout this letter we see Paul model humility. Instead of commanding Philemon to reconcile with Onesimus, he makes an appeal as "an old man and now a prisoner." Yet, the gentle tone of his appeal might leave the wrong impression that reconciliation is optional. This is not at all the case. Even in the Lord's prayer we plead, "forgive us our debts, as we also have forgiven our debtors" (Matthew 6:12). In Ephesians 4:32 Paul writes: "Be kind to one another, tenderhearted, forgiving one another, as God in Christ forgave you." Through the Parable of the Unforgiving Servant, Jesus says: "And should not you have had mercy on your fellow servant, as I had mercy on you?" (Matthew 18:33). During conflicts, it is helpful to remember the phrase "do what is required": reconciliation is a mandate, not an option.

At the same time, Paul expresses here and elsewhere his concern for what we could call "heart-change." For example, in 2 Corinthians 9:7 Paul writes: "Each one must give as he has decided in his heart, not reluctantly or under compulsion, for God loves a cheerful giver." The apostle is not suggesting that we should give tithes and offerings only when we have attained cheerful hearts. If anything, God often uses "mechanical" obedience to change us. The gospel, however, is concerned not just with behavioral change but also—and primarily—with heart-change. Thus, we should forgive because that is what God requires from us; but we should also forgive "for love's sake," that is, as people who have been loved in order to love.

Prayer

Jesus, my king, I too often treat reconciliation as if it were an option or a matter of convenience. Thank you for your Word that reminds me "to do what is required." More so, thank you for the ways your Word points me continually to the heart, teaching me that any behavioral change must be rooted in the sort of deep change that only the gospel can bring. Give me strength to do what I must; but in the process, change my heart that I might love and embrace my enemies as you have loved and embraced me. Amen.

Day 12

Philemon 10a

"I appeal to you for my child"

Many view conflict (and life, for that matter) as a private affair. If those two people are in conflict, there's no reason for me to get involved. This way of thinking is consistent with the popular mantra, "Live and let live." And to some degree we should refrain from being busybodies. Yet, as we see in the situation between Onesimus and Philemon, reconciliation is sometimes impossible without a mediator. Knowing this, Paul decides to make an "appeal" on behalf of his "child."

The work of mediation is messy. No one knew this better than our Lord Jesus Christ. In 1 Timothy 2:5–6, Paul writes: "For there is one God, and there is one mediator between God and men, the man Christ Jesus, who gave himself as a ransom for all, which is the testimony given at the proper time." By serving as the "mediator between God and men," Jesus was ultimately killed for the ones he came to save. We also know how much he suffered during his earthly ministry.

We must ask, "What does it mean for us to follow our Lord Jesus Christ?" After all, if Jesus told us, "A servant is not greater than his master" (John 15:20), and if Jesus committed himself to the hard work of reconciliation on the cross, what does this mean for us who confess him as Lord and Savior? To be sure, the work of mediation requires much patience and wisdom. There is also the danger of falling into the sinful complex of "needing to be needed." But all this is what we must endure in order to serve as ambassadors of God and agents of reconciliation.

Prayer

God, there are conflicts in my life that do not directly involve me. For a variety of reasons, I've chosen not to get involved. Mediation is almost always a messy affair. But the life and ministry of Jesus remind me of the kind of life you have called me to pursue as an ambassador of peace. Give me courage to do what you require and wisdom to discern how to facilitate reconciliation in complicated and heated situations. Amen.

Day 13

Philemon 10b–11

> "Onesimus, whose father I became in my imprisonment. (Formerly he was useless to you, but now he is indeed useful to you and to me.)"

A KEY PART OF reconciliation is helping persons in conflict to gain perspective. In the current situation, Philemon's perspective is fairly narrow: Onesimus has wronged him, so Philemon wants nothing to do with him. Paul therefore wants to shed new light on who Onesimus has become.

Paul refers to Onesimus as his "child" (v. 10a) because he came to faith through Paul's ministry. A literal translation of the Greek in verse 10b reads, "whom I begot in my chains, Onesimus." Somehow the two had connected, and during their time together Onesimus converted. This conversion meant that Onesimus was no longer an object of God's wrath but a child of the living God, fully forgiven and welcomed. This also meant that Onesimus and Paul were now part of the same family, with Paul as his spiritual "father." The apostle seeks to highlight the significance of Onesimus's conversion through the use of "Formerly . . . but now" language. Onesimus is now a fundamentally different person. Neither Paul nor Philemon can view him in the same way.

In what sense is Onesimus now "useful" to Philemon? Paul later answers this question in verse 13: "I would have been glad to keep him with me, in order that he might serve me on your behalf during my imprisonment for the gospel." As is often the case, converts experience a new sense of joy, focus, and purpose. We can assume this is what happened with Onesimus. In effect, Philemon's bondservant Onesimus has been serving Philemon's fellow worker (v. 1) and thus bringing honor to God. Paul's hope is that Philemon would recognize the profound good that has taken place in and through Onesimus—despite the situation—and thus soften in his disposition toward him.

Prayer

Father in heaven, I confess that in conflict too often I reduce people to their sins or see them solely through the ways they have hurt me. They cease to be full persons with strengths and weaknesses and become offenders who deserve nothing but my wrath. Move me to pray for my enemies. Through your Spirit's softening and the help of my church community, give me a wider perspective on the person and the situation. Help me to see beyond my personal grievance that I might appreciate the good you are accomplishing. Amen.

Day 14

Philemon 12

"I am sending him back to you, sending my very heart"

THE RELATIONSHIP BETWEEN PAUL and Onesimus represents the most unlikely of relationships. Paul was a Jew, Onesimus a Gentile. Paul was educated, a Pharisee among Pharisees, Onesimus a slave. As a Roman citizen, Paul had rights, Onesimus had few, if any. And contrary to what some might believe, Paul was not all that different from us. Originally, he fraternized only with those who were similar to him. How, then, does he reach a point of considering Onesimus his "child" (v. 10), his "very heart" (v. 12)? As noted earlier (v. 7), in the Bible the "heart" represents a person's essence. Thus, by referring to Onesimus as his "very heart," Paul is indicating that Onesimus has become a close and helpful companion.

In Galatians 3:28, Paul writes: "There is neither Jew nor Greek, there is neither slave nor free, there is no male and female, for you are all one in Christ Jesus." The gospel levels out the playing field by declaring that "all have sinned and fall short of the glory of God, and are justified by his grace as a gift, through the redemption that is in Christ Jesus" (Romans 3:23–24). Previously, a person's physical, moral, spiritual, or professional accomplishments functioned as dividing walls. Now, however, such walls have crumbled down because none can say he or she is better than another. All have sinned and all are saved by the kindness and favor of God, which are freely offered to us offered in Christ Jesus. Therefore, in Christ all are one and free to enjoy deep relationships that would have otherwise been impossible. This is Paul's hope for Philemon, that he too would eventually count Onesimus as his "very heart."

Prayer

Father in heaven, thank you for adopting me into your family. Prior to coming to faith, I fraternized only with those who were similar to me. I spoke, ate, and spent time with people most similar to me. Moreover, I confess that such things became the basis for feeling superior to others. But I believe in the gospel that says all believers are the same—justified sinners through faith in Christ Jesus. Bring this belief into fruition by creating new relationships that reflect the transforming power of the gospel. Amen.

Day 15

Philemon 13–14a

> "I would have been glad to keep him with me, in order that he might serve me on your behalf during my imprisonment for the gospel, but I preferred to do nothing without your consent"

To understand verses 13–14a, we need to go back and make a general observation. In verse 12, Paul writes: "I am sending him back to you, sending my very heart." But as Paul now makes clear in verses 13–14a, "I would have been glad to keep him . . . but I preferred to do nothing without your consent." It is not that Onesimus volunteered to return to Philemon (though we shouldn't assume he was opposed to the idea); rather, Paul decided to send him back even if this meant bidding farewell to his "very heart." Similarly, Paul indicates that he very much wanted to keep Onesimus with him during his "imprisonment for the gospel"; but, more so, he wanted to honor Philemon by considering first his preference. This is noteworthy, given their spiritual father-son relationship in which Paul had led Philemon to faith (v. 19). It would have been more fitting for Philemon to sacrifice for his imprisoned "father."

So why does Paul decide to "take the hit"? He is modeling Philippians 2:4: "Let each of you look not only to his own interests, but also to the interests of others." This is what Christ has done for us. Jesus "did not count equality with God a thing to be grasped, but emptied himself, by taking the form of a servant" and dying on the cross in our place (Philippians 2:6–8). By sending his "very heart"—despite Onesimus's invaluable service—Paul was imitating Jesus by giving up his preference and convenience for the sake of another. This is the very thing he will ask of Philemon—to surrender what might be owed to him for the sake of Onesimus and the church that meets in his house. This doesn't mean we should never pursue justice and in some cases reparations. But in personal conflict, what is often necessary is looking to the interests of others—not only the offender but also the broader community—above your own in order to make peace. Thanks be to God who makes this possible by giving us the mind of Christ.

Prayer

Lord Jesus, thank you for surrendering your rights in order to reconcile God and humanity. If you had clung to what was owed to you, what hope would I have? In conflict I get so preoccupied with how I have been offended that I fail to consider the needs of others above my own. Give me wisdom to discern when it is fitting to surrender my "rights" in order to advance reconciliation. Grant me faith to believe that in the end you will right every wrong. May this conviction free me to become an instrument of peace, for your glory. Amen.

Day 16

Philemon 14b

"in order that your goodness might not be by compulsion but of your own accord"

THE FIRST HALF OF verse 14 reads: "but I preferred to do nothing without your consent." The Greek term for "consent" could also be translated "decision," "resolve," or "intention." The second half of verse 14 clarifies what Paul has in mind through the contrast between "compulsion" and "your own accord." Whatever "goodness" Philemon does, Paul wants it to be the result of a decision he has made—not because of an obligation imposed on him by the apostle (vv. 8–9). To be sure, early in the Christian life, when a person is still young in his or her faith and lacks a strong grasp of the Bible, it is wise to submit to the guidance of the leadership. But as a person matures, obedience should also come from a personal resolve to carry out core biblical convictions.[1] Here, Paul wants Philemon to make a decision to receive Onesimus based on Philemon's own convictions concerning the meaning of Christian fellowship (v. 6). This is what it means to become mature in Christ.

Verse 14 also reminds us that reconciliation often begins with a decision rather than a feeling. I suspect this is what Jesus

---

1. Wright, *Epistles*, 184: "This is the nature of Paul's authority 'in Christ': it is a healing, creative responsibility which, by setting out the facts of the case, theologically, practically and pastorally, invites Christians to work out the proper conclusions in belief and practice."

had in mind when he commanded his disciples to "pray for those who persecute you" (Matthew 5:44), or what Paul had in mind when he echoed the proverb, "if your enemy is hungry, feed him; if he is thirsty, give him something to drink" (Romans 12:20). Neither command requires an innate desire to pray for and feed our enemies. If loving, forgiving, and embracing those who have offended us depended solely on any change on their end, the likelihood of reconciliation would be close to none. Similarly, if making peace depended on any change on your end, specifically having warm and positive feelings toward your enemy, broken relationships would persist. Verse 14, therefore, is a fitting reminder that reconciliation will often require us to make a resolution to love and forgive irrespective of how we feel or how little our offenders change. Such a resolution stems from the reality and command to be kind and forgiving as God in Christ has forgiven us (Ephesians 4:32).

Prayer

Gracious and loving Father, your will is for me to mature into the likeness of your Son. This entails studying and meditating on the Bible and forming deep convictions on the kind of life you want me to pursue. Thank you for this sobering reminder that reconciliation often requires a resolve on my part to love, forgive, and embrace others irrespective of how I feel or whether my enemy changes. Fix my eyes on the kindness and forgiveness you have given me in Christ so that I might have sufficient grace to love and pray for my enemies. Amen.

Day 17

Philemon 15

"For this perhaps is why he was parted from you for a while,
that you might have him back forever"

AS NOTED ALREADY, FACILITATING peace often depends on helping offended parties gain perspective on a given situation. Right now, all Philemon sees is how Onesimus has hurt him, and so he's unwilling to forgive. Verse 15 invites Philemon to take a step back and consider the situation from an eternal perspective. To be sure, the apostle is cautious about speaking on God's behalf (this is why he uses the adverb "perhaps"). Nevertheless, as the "divine passive" suggests ("he was parted from you"), Paul is sure that God is in control and has been working good.

The new perspective Paul wants Philemon to adopt is best understood through the contrast between "a while" and "forever." Paul doesn't mean to minimize whatever loss Philemon has suffered. Yet, eternity does have a unique way of putting things in perspective. In the next verse Paul will specify the gains Philemon now enjoys as a result of Onesimus's conversion. For now, he is simply asking Philemon to consider how God has worked good in a situation that only seemed bad—God saved Onesimus "forever" despite the unfavorable circumstances leading up to his conversion. However much Philemon has suffered "for a while" pales in comparison to the eternal good God has accomplished. Any refusal to receive Onesimus suggests that Onesimus's offense against Philemon is weightier than the good God has accomplished.

Viewing conflict in this way is difficult. It doesn't come naturally. It requires sacrifice. It also requires "real" belief in God's sovereignty. But God promises grace to those who resolve to surrender their present sufferings for the sake of God's eternal purposes.

Prayer

Gracious Father, I find rest in knowing that you are sovereign over every situation and always working good. Sometimes I can see the good you're doing, sometimes I can't. Even so, whether I am able to see the good, I want to make decisions according to an eternal perspective. Help me to consider not just the ways I have been hurt but also—and perhaps more so—the ways I can bring you most glory by pursuing peace with all my might. Amen.

Day 18

Philemon 16

"no longer as a bondservant but more than a bondservant, as a beloved brother—especially to me, but how much more to you, both in the flesh and in the Lord"

FAMILY. COMPLICATED. PLAIN AND simple. To be sure, great in so many ways but definitely complicated. We've heard it said, "Never mix family and business," but this is the situation Philemon now faces. Life was easier—it was more straightforward—when Onesimus was just a "bondservant." But now, as a result of his conversion, Onesimus is "more than a bondservant"—he is "a beloved brother." Earlier, in verse 1, Paul referred to Philemon as a "beloved fellow worker." It's not by accident that he uses the same language here to describe Onesimus. In doing so, he is making clear that from the apostle's perspective the two are the same "in the Lord": they belong to the same spiritual family, they are both loved by God and the apostle, and they share the same mission to make disciples of all nations.

What does it mean for Philemon now to relate to Onesimus as a "beloved brother . . . both in the flesh and in the Lord"? Does Paul simply mean that Philemon is to treat him better than he would have otherwise? Or does he mean something more? Could Paul be hinting at his desire to see Philemon release Onesimus as a bondservant so that Onesimus could now be both a beloved and freed brother? Characteristic of Paul in this letter, the apostle doesn't provide such explicit directives. Yet, in verse 6, he prays that Philemon would come to discern every good thing God intends as he lives in fellowship with other believers. It is not at all a stretch that Paul was hoping that Philemon would connect the dots, that even if it meant financial sacrifice, Philemon would release Onesimus from enslavement. By doing so, Philemon would be walking in step with the gospel, realizing for Onesimus in the present age what was already true for him in eternity, namely his freedom in Christ Jesus.

Those who have hurt us become our debtors. At the very least, they owe us an apology. In most cases, they owe us more. Verse 16 encourages us to free our debtors—to do the complicated and sacrificial work of forgiveness—because of the new reality God has established according to the gospel.

Prayer

Father in heaven, I confess that sometimes I want just you and not your family. But I know there is little possibility for personal growth unless I give the very things I have received—forgiveness, grace, and generosity. As I continue to live in deep fellowship with other believers, help me to discern and do the complicated and sacrificial good works that you have planned in advance for me. Help me to be especially deliberate about walking in step with the gospel when it comes to the important task of seeking reconciliation. Amen.

Day 19

Philemon 17

> "So if you consider me your partner, receive him as you would receive me"

THE APOSTLE FINALLY EXPRESSES directly the purpose of his letter. Verse 17—and the several concrete commands that follow—reminds us to guard against the error of reflection without action.

On the one hand, Paul wants Philemon to consider everything he has said so far in the letter ("So") but especially their common fellowship in Christ Jesus ("partner"). Philemon is to consider the fact that his beloved fellow worker is a prisoner for Christ Jesus (vv. 1, 9); he is to consider the impact he has had on all the saints and the impact his decision regarding Onesimus will have on them (vv. 2, 5, 7); he is to consider what God is calling him to do as he lives in deep fellowship with other believers (v. 6); he is to consider reconciliation as that which is required of anyone that has been reconciled to God through Christ (v. 8); he is to consider Onesimus's new state as a converted person, now a beloved child to Paul and brother to Philemon (vv. 10–12, 16); and he is to consider that perhaps God has been working good despite all the evil.

On the other hand, Paul doesn't want Philemon to spend all his time in deep reflection. In the end, the letter is a call to action—Paul's point being, "In view of all this, receive Onesimus." Moreover, Paul isn't just asking Philemon to grudgingly coexist with Onesimus. He's asking for something much more radical:

"receive him as you would receive me." Later Paul expresses how he himself expects to be treated: "prepare a guest room for me" (v. 22). This would have entailed not just a bed but also hospitality—food, drink, conversation, and so forth. Given Onesimus is now Paul's child in the faith and Philemon's "beloved brother," the only fitting course of action would be to embrace Onesimus with the same kind of tenderness and generosity he would show Paul. All in all, verse 17 is a summons to "be doers of the word, and not hearers only, deceiving yourselves" (James 1:22).

Prayer

Almighty God, thank you for the wisdom and insight you have given through your Word. You desire for me to grow in wisdom, to be thoughtful about how I interpret life, and to be purposeful in all my decisions. You also desire for me to be not just a thinker of your Word but also a doer. Guard me from the twin errors of thoughtlessness and inaction. Make me complete like your Son who knew your Word and obeyed it perfectly to effect reconciliation. Give me strength now to embrace those who are my brothers and sisters in Christ. Amen.

Day 20

Philemon 18

> "If he has wronged you at all, or owes you anything,
> charge that to my account"

Now that Paul has finally made clear his appeal (v. 17), he wants to make sure that Philemon does "what is required" (v. 8). Verse 18 seems to advance Paul's efforts by addressing the issue of what is owed to Philemon. However, it also raises at least two questions.

First, Paul begins with the conditional "If." He neither denies nor affirms that Onesimus has "wronged" Philemon. Clearly, something has happened, something so catastrophic that the two had to be separated. But Paul decides not to take a clear stance. This might have been his way of saying in verse 18, "At this point, what's more important than assigning blame is reconciling. To that end, I'll cover whatever might be owed to Philemon." Second, we can't help but wonder how Paul was going to pay the debt. Does Paul have access to a large sum of money or income stream despite his imprisonment? Is he planning to work after being freed from his imprisonment?

While we shouldn't doubt the sincerity of Paul's offer, I suspect that the words "charge that to my account" were meant to remind Philemon of the gospel. In 2 Corinthians 5:20–21, Paul writes: "We implore you on behalf of Christ, be reconciled to God. For our sake he made him to be sin who knew no sin, so that in him we might become the righteousness of God." The gospel doesn't say,

"If we have wronged God . . ."; rather, that "all have sinned and fall short of the glory of God" (Romans 3:23). There was, then, a debt owed to God that we could never repay. But Christ Jesus came and declared, "Charge that to my account." On the cross, payment for our debt was made so that in Christ we might be freed and counted righteous. The parallel between what Paul intends to do and what Christ did is undeniable. Verse 18 is likely a subtle reminder to Philemon of the grace he has received. This grace, in turn, should shape his response to his supposed transgressor.

Prayer

Lord Jesus, you taught us to pray, "forgive us our debts, as we also have forgiven our debtors" (Matthew 6:12). I confess that I want grace but fail to extend grace. In all my conflicts bring to mind the glorious gospel. I have become righteous because my wrongs were charged to you. I did not receive what was owed to me because you Lord received what was not owed to you. Let this wondrous reality reshape the way I handle conflict, for your glory. Amen.

Day 21

Philemon 19

"I, Paul, write this with my own hand:
I will repay it—to say nothing of your owing me even your own self"

WE ARE ALL DEBTORS. We are debtors to Christ Jesus who became sin for us so that in him we might become God's righteousness. We are also debtors to those who have labored so that we might come to believe in the gospel. I am a debtor to my Sunday School teacher who taught me the Bible for several years and prayed for me when many others had given up on me. I am a debtor to my parents who have embodied what it means to live all of life—including "retirement"—unto the Lord. Here, while Paul reiterates that he "will repay" whatever might be owed to Philemon by Onesimus, his main point is that Philemon is a debtor to the apostle: "to say nothing of your owing me even your own self." The statement likely means that Philemon came to faith through Paul's ministry. In this sense, everything that Philemon now is and enjoys in Christ is because of Paul.

Recognizing this, Philemon should adopt a favorable disposition toward Onesimus for the sake of his spiritual father. When David finds Mephibosheth, the son of his dear friend, he says, "Do not fear, for I will show you kindness for the sake of your father Jonathan" (2 Samuel 9:7). When God the Father looks at us, he treats us as his beloved children for the sake of Christ. When we forgive and embrace believers that have wronged us, we do so out of reverence for God, who first loved and forgave us. This is especially important to keep in mind when we don't feel any natural desire toward reconciliation. For the sake of the gospel and as debtors to grace, we are to do the things we don't want to do because Christ our Lord declares, "to say nothing of your owing me even your own self."

Prayer

Great God of highest heaven, thank you for reminding me that I myself am a debtor to grace. I am a child of God because your Son was cast out. I am a believer because another shared the gospel with me in word and deed. Mature me to go beyond how I feel to what I owe: I owe it to you to forgive as I have been forgiven, to love my enemies because you pursued rebels to your will. And I trust that you will take my dutiful obedience to create a sincere love for my enemies. Amen.

Day 22

Philemon 20

"Yes, brother, I want some benefit from you in the Lord.
Refresh my heart in Christ"

WITH VERSE 20, PAUL begins to conclude the letter. This is signaled through the repetition of key terms that occurred in v. 7, the prelude to the body of the letter, where Paul said: "For I have derived much joy and comfort from your love, my *brother*, because the *hearts* of the saints have been *refreshed* through you."

As is fitting with any conclusion, Paul reiterates his main burden in the letter—to facilitate unity among those who are "in the Lord" and "in Christ" (notice its repetition in verse 20). He does this by calling to mind all the main characters. First, he refers directly to Philemon as "brother." Then he refers to himself through the pronoun "I." (In Greek, the explicit mention of the personal pronoun is gratuitous. When included, it is usually emphatic; thus, "*I myself* want some benefit from you in the Lord.") But what about Onesimus? Scholars have noted Paul's use of the verb "want some benefit," which occurs only here in the New Testament. The verb transliterates as *oninēmi*, which of course looks eerily similar to the name Onesimus. It is improbable that this is mere coincidence. As he prepares to conclude the letter, the apostle wants to identify subtly but clearly all who are family "in the Lord."[1]

---

1. As noted already, Paul's use of the verb "refresh" echoes verse 7. In this earlier verse, Paul brings attention to how Philemon has encouraged all the

Striking about verse 20 is Paul's use of the command, "Refresh my heart," given up to this point he has adopted the tone of an appeal (v. 8). More than pointing to his own apostolic authority, the command points to the lordship of Christ and the obligations that come from being in the fellowship of believers (v. 6). Human tendency is to look first to one's own needs. The summons of the gospel is to seek first the welfare of others, even as Jesus considered our needs above his own. The Letter to Philemon is a perennial reminder to go and do likewise—to refresh the hearts of all those who are one "in the Lord."

Prayer

Lord Jesus, on earth you made this radical declaration: "Who is my mother, and who are my brothers? . . . For whoever does the will of my Father in heaven is my brother and sister and mother" (Matthew 12:48–50). In yourself you radically redefine family, transcending traditional boundaries of race, class, and education. Your family includes even those who abandoned and mocked you—your enemies. Help me to have a new attitude that embraces all who are in you, and help me to be intentional in all that I do, always seeking to refresh the hearts of all the saints. Amen.

---

saints that meet in his house. The verb's occurrence in verse 20 may be a subtle reminder of all the saints that will be impacted by Philemon's decision to reconcile (or not) moving forward.

Day 23

Philemon 21

"Confident of your obedience, I write to you, knowing that you will do even more than I say"

"Obedience" has fallen out of fashion. What's more important than submission to any external person or law is being true to the self: at the end of life, I want to be able to say, "I did it my way." The Christian life is also about freedom, but a different sort. It's about freedom from bitterness and selfishness. It's about freedom to love and embrace beyond our natural boundaries and preferences. The kind of "obedience" that Paul has in mind in verse 21 is not slavish conformity to a rigid set of religious rules, but a joyful devotion to the One that has freed us and brought us into his family.

Even though Paul has adopted the stance of an old father making an appeal to his beloved son, in verse 21 he makes clear that they are dealing with a mandate, a command to reconcile. Throughout this letter Paul has not focused on his apostolic authority but on the fellowship that all believers share in Christ and the demands that come with it. Elsewhere in Paul's letters he uses the phrase "obedience of faith" (e.g., Romans 1:5). By faith we believe that we are free from the power of sin and death. By faith we believe that someday we will reign with Christ in glory. But this same faith brings with it duties and demands, not dissimilar to the obligations that come with marriage and parenting. In this sense, the Letter to Philemon is a reminder to submit to the law of freedom, the law of love. It's an exhortation to recall and obey the mandate to be reconciled.

One way to discern whether we are living in the freedom of the gospel is to ask whether we are doing the bare minimum or "even more than I say." That is, when we love somebody (our spouse, our children, even our pet), our disposition is not to do as little as possible. Instead, we think regularly about the ones we love and seek ways to express our care and affection for them. Paul's expectation of Philemon is more than an internal decision to forgive. It's even more than general friendliness. While Paul doesn't outright say, "Free Onesimus from the bonds of slavery," this seems implied in his words, "I write to you, knowing that you will do even more than I say." Christ, after all, did not do the bare minimum for his brothers and sisters—he gave it all for their freedom. Our Lord trusts that we will do the same, that we will do even more than he asks for our new family.

Prayer

Father in heaven, thank you for saving me and bringing me into your family. Help me to remember that I am your child and, as your child, I am under the law of love. More than being true to myself, enable me to be true to you by loving and embracing my brothers and sisters in the Lord. And as I consider Christ, who did more than what was required, may I learn to do likewise. I know all this is possible through your Spirit. Amen.

Day 24

Philemon 22

"At the same time, prepare a guest room for me, for I am hoping that through your prayers I will be graciously given to you"

Almost everyone agrees that accountability is a good thing, but few people practice it because—almost always—awkward situations arise. At best, we'll ask evasive questions like, "Are you seeking to become more gracious," versus direct questions like, "Did you reconcile with your spouse yet?" We would prefer to avoid situations where failures need to be admitted or heard.

Paul, however, understood that rarely do people change without accountability. This is why he says to Philemon, "prepare a guest room for me." Paul intends to come and see whether Philemon has done the very things he has asked. He could have, of course, inquired via letter whether Philemon had decided to receive Onesimus. But he understood the power (and pressure) of personal presence: he knew it would be far more difficult for Philemon to continue in disobedience with Paul's bodily and prolonged presence. The request, then, in the first half of verse 22 is a subtle indication of the apostle's resolve to hold Philemon accountable.

The second half of the verse is not just an expression of Paul's desire to be freed from imprisonment. It is another attempt to identify with Onesimus, who remains a debtor to Philemon. The Greek verb translated as "graciously given" carries the connotations of being pardoned for a wrong or being forgiven of a debt.

Paul's use of the verb here seems deliberate. As he did in verse 1 by adopting the title "prisoner," so now he again identifies with Onesimus by expressing their shared desire—to be freed and "graciously given to you," no longer as marginalized prisoners but as fully received members of God's household.

Prayer

God, thank you for surrounding me with brothers and sisters who make mutual accountability possible. Help me to love them enough to encourage them to live in a way that honors you. Help me to be humble enough to receive their encouragement and even their rebukes. Finally, soften my heart and show me concrete ways I can identify with those who live on the fringes. As your Son identified with my frailty and as Paul identified with Onesimus, help me to love and embrace those who are neglected even within your household. Let me reflect the mercy you have given me. Amen.

Day 25

Philemon 23–24

"Epaphras, my fellow prisoner in Christ Jesus, sends greetings to you, and so do Mark, Aristarchus, Demas, and Luke, my fellow workers"[1]

THERE'S A FINE LINE between peer pressure and accountability. Usually peer pressure involves something bad—a prank, the use of illegal substances, participation in bullying, and so forth. Accountability (in the Christian sense) is calling other believers to walk in step with the gospel. In individualistic cultures where religion has become privatized, Christian accountability has all but disappeared, having degenerated into irregular exchanges of superficial questions. Many have come to believe that we should neither give nor receive any "pressure" to do good. This belief has stripped us of one of our most basic God-given means for maturing in Christ.

Verses 23–24 are more than just exchanges between believers. The Letter to Philemon was a publicly read document. Thus verse 21, "Confident of your obedience, I write to you, knowing that you will do even more than I say," would have been heard by all the believers with Philemon. The apostle was placing public pressure on Philemon. Similarly, the mention of Epaphras, Mark,

---

1. The "you" in verse 23 is singular whereas "your" in verse 22 was plural. (For most of the letter, Paul is addressing the singular "you," i.e., Philemon.) This abrupt shift from the plural (v. 22) to the singular (v. 23) brings focus back to Philemon, in effect: "The brothers greet *you*, the brothers who are fully aware of the situation and who are also confident of your obedience to my appeal."

Aristarchus, Demas, and Luke, fellow prisoners and workers, is deliberate. Paul is conveying that all of Philemon's colleagues have been made aware of the situation. This alone would have added pressure on Philemon "to do what is required" (v. 8). As we can see, Paul was serious about obedience and, thus, serious about accountability. He was supremely confident in a person's inability to change left to him or herself.

Philemon was a leader among the believers. He was generous and hospitable. His ministry regularly refreshed the saints. Yet even he needed further exhortation and accountability. If this was true for him, how much more must this be true for us today?

Prayer

Jesus, teach me that wisdom rests in underestimating my ability to overcome sin on my own. Forgive me for acknowledging the importance of accountability but failing to pursue it. My failure is an expression of my pride. I admit that I am naturally averse to the pressures of obedience, but this is what I need—and what you have generously given—for my sanctification. Convict me now to make use of this means of grace, that I might become more like Christ. Amen.

Day 26

Philemon 24

"and so do Mark, Aristarchus, Demas, and Luke, my fellow workers"

A FEW VERSES FROM Acts illuminate the significance of including "Mark" in the final greetings:

> Now Barnabas wanted to take with them John called Mark. But Paul thought best not to take with them one who had withdrawn from them in Pamphylia and had not gone with them to the work. And there arose a sharp disagreement, so that they separated from each other. (Acts 15:37–39)

In some ways, the apostle was superhuman. He survived multiple beatings, several shipwrecks, and even a stoning. Despite all this suffering, he never turned his back on his calling to preach the gospel. Yet, in some ways, he was ordinary. He too knew how to nurse a grudge. He too had little tolerance for unreliable people. Thus, when Mark, who had basically flaked on Paul and Barnabas, wanted to join them on another missionary journey, Paul refused. The bitter disagreement between him and Barnabas suggests that Paul's reasons were just as much personal as they were "professional."

But Paul also knew a thing about mercy. In one of his final letters, he writes:

> I thank him who has given me strength, Christ Jesus our Lord, because he judged me faithful, appointing me to his service, though formerly I was a blasphemer, persecutor, and insolent opponent. But I received mercy because I had acted ignorantly in unbelief, and the grace of our Lord overflowed for me with the faith and love that are in Christ Jesus. (1 Timothy 1:12–14)

In short, Paul had received mercy. He had proven that he was a failure. And what was God's response? He enlisted Paul to serve as his ambassador to the Gentiles. Unsurprisingly, this personal gospel reality enabled Paul to forgive and receive Mark anew as a "fellow worker." By including Mark in these closing greetings, Paul was reminding Philemon that the apostle himself had to learn how to extend the same grace all Christians have received in Christ Jesus.

Prayer

Father in heaven, it both humbles and challenges me to know that even the "super apostle" had to learn how to show grace. If someone as inspired and devoted as Paul struggled in this way—and yet made every effort to reconcile—how much more must I seek to forgive and embrace believers that have wronged me. Turn my eyes to Jesus. Let me look upon the crown of thorns and his pierced hands and feet, so that I might know what it took for me to be reconciled to you. May the grace I have received empower me to embrace all who profess faith in Christ. Amen.

Day 27

Philemon 25

"The grace of the Lord Jesus Christ be with your spirit"

THE CLOSING REMARKS IN Moo's commentary are most fitting here:

> Since this grace wish is so much a staple of Paul's letter closings, it might be that he adds it here without giving it much thought. But we might wonder whether Paul could ever write about grace without thinking about its significance. And here he might especially be aware of how much the whole community would need a strong measure of grace in order to respond well to the Onesimus affair.[1]

God's empowering grace is needed from beginning to end, as the double occurrence of grace at the beginning (v. 3) and conclusion (v. 25) of the letter suggests.[2] Such "grace" comes from God—not from ourselves, not by "looking within"—so that in the end he might receive all glory. Our persistent refusal to do what is right and necessary—in the case of Philemon, to make peace with Onesimus—should point us away from ourselves. The Bible promises

---

1. Moo, *Letters*, 422.

2. Wright, *Epistles*, 192: "The conventional tone of the closing greeting, once again, should not blind us to the truth it conveys to us, and the power that the expressed prayer conveyed to Philemon. It is a hard thing Paul has asked of him: a superhuman task of heartfelt reconciliation and forgiveness. If he is to do it without pride or anger, he cannot do it without grace."

that grace is given to those who humble themselves by turning to God for grace to do what is required.

May "the grace of the Lord Jesus Christ be with your spirit" as you seek to make peace for his glory!

Prayer

Lord Jesus Christ, thank you for promising to be with me until the very end of the age (Matthew 28:20). Thank you for your Spirit who enables me to be and do what I cannot left to myself. Thank you for the Letter to Philemon that reminds me of my familial obligations as a member of your household. Give me wisdom and grace as I seek to become a peacemaker for your glory. Amen.

Summary

Reflections and Resolutions

Philemon was a leader among the believers who met in his house. His life was so commendable, marked especially by generosity and inspirational leadership, that even the apostle Paul admired him. Similarly, Paul was an apostle of apostles, considered today as the primary shaper of the Christian faith second to Jesus. Yet, for Philemon and Paul, reconciliation came naturally to neither one of these spiritual gurus. Rather, they had to learn to forgive and embrace those who had wronged them through deep theological reflection and deliberate decision. All this reminds us that though we possess the Spirit of Christ and are a new creation in him, many Christian duties do not arise spontaneously. They must be learned and nurtured through the reminders and accountability of other believers.

Striking is the implicit juxtaposition: Philemon doesn't struggle with sharing his money, but he can't extend forgiveness to Onesimus. This is noteworthy because many believers—even the sincerest ones—are not generous with their resources. They fail to tithe and open their homes to share meals with believers and unbelievers alike. Philemon, however, doesn't struggle with this, which indicates that he is mature as a believer. Yet, he can't forgive and embrace. This juxtaposition is at least suggestive of the profound grip that pride and bitterness can have on us: we have a hard time forgiving those that have—in our eyes—personally wronged us.[1]

Few Christians would deny the importance of reconciliation in the Christian faith. God has reconciled us to himself in Christ and calls us to be reconciled to each other. Jesus himself underscored the priority that reconciliation should have in the life of believers: "So if you are offering your gift at the altar and there remember that your brother has something against you, leave your gift there before the altar and go. First be reconciled to your brother, and then come and offer your gift" (Matthew 5:23-24). Yet, even with all this clarity, the call to create a culture of peace seems all but lost in many churches today.[2] Sadly, this is often justified, as was perhaps the case with Philemon, in the name of ministry: we busy ourselves with preparing sermons, serving as small group leaders, participating in soup kitchens—as we should—while neglecting what Jesus considers the more basic task to "go" and "be reconciled to your brother." Eventually, consciously or not, we convince ourselves that "God understands" we can't do everything and that reconciliation might happen if the opportunity presents itself. In short, we become passive participants instead of proactive pursuers of peace.

The desire to reconcile is as foreign as wanting to get our teeth cleaned at the dentist. Like exercise, we recognize its importance, but somehow it gets lost among our priorities. Over against this reality, the Letter to Philemon challenges followers of Christ, especially those who like Philemon are in positions of influence and are busying themselves with good works, to remember that they belong to the family of Christ. As such, they need to think through the implications of their actions and inactions. In the case of Philemon, how will his refusal to receive another brother in the Lord affect the community of faith? Will it contribute to creating a

---

1. While I speak of this inability to forgive due to pride, it is also on account of a sense of justice. When a person wrongs us, they owe us—they become our debtors. Our refusal to forgive and embrace does represent, to some degree, an outworking of a natural and right desire to see justice.

2. For further reflections on this specific point, see my comments in *Unreconciled*.

culture where being "unreconciled" becomes the norm? Will such failure to extend grace despite the message of grace cause some to stumble and even leave the faith? While we often view reconciliation as a personal matter, the Letter to Philemon reminds us that it is exactly the opposite: reconciliation between two persons ultimately involves and impacts larger communities.

Reflection over such questions isn't meant to take place in the realm of theory. Verse 6, which is probably the most pivotal verse in the letter, teaches that insight into God's will for our lives comes as we engage in deep and regular fellowship with believers. In other words, if we choose to remain at a distance by adopting the religion of "God and me," the sort of spirituality that steers clear of "institutionalized religion," we will likely remain ignorant of how to steward our lives for God's glory. This is the plain and simple reality that verse 6 underscores: if we're serious about living for his glory, we need to get serious about integrating ourselves into a church that is committed to the gospel. In this sense, the Letter to Philemon is a summons to adopt a familial mindset, to no longer make decisions on the basis of personality and preference, but to pursue courses of action that strengthen the family of God.

While writing this devotional, I read Jeannette Walls's *New York Times* bestseller *The Glass Castle: A Memoir*. Walls narrates beautifully the joys, complexities, and brokenness of her upbringing, much of which she better realized as an adult. It would be uncharitable to say that her parents failed to love her and her siblings. Moreover, Walls's story of her family helps us to see the idols of our own families, whether by contrast or parallelism. Still, one can't escape the feeling that her parents regularly made decisions that led to undue suffering on the part of the children. Rather than doing what was best for the family, they often made decisions to fulfill their own desires and aspirations. The brokenness that followed illustrates the consequences of failing to adopt a familial outlook on life. For this reason, it's worthwhile to add verse 6 of Philemon to our cache of memory verses (John 3:16 would fall into that bucket) that are basic for the Christian life. This verse, as we have indicated regularly in the devotional, is especially relevant given our individualistic impulse.

The Letter to Philemon is also a model par excellence of winsome mediation. Speaking the truth in love is often mistaken as a license for "just being real" and "saying things as they are." I plead guilty. Often, I speak from a place of frustration and anger instead of wisdom and patience.

Conflicts are often marked by pride, bitterness, and a resolve to hold on to anger. Apart from mediation, warring parties may never reconcile. This is why other Christians need to get involved, even if this means stepping into the inevitable messiness that will follow. Where would we be if Christ had opted to remain at a safe distance instead of stepping into creation and achieving reconciliation through his blood, sweat, tears, and ultimately his death? So mediation is absolutely necessary for building cultures of peace. But such mediation must exhibit the character of wisdom Paul models in this letter.

Some aspects of Paul's winsome mediation are worth highlighting. First, he lays the groundwork of relationship. There can be no doubt that Paul is relying heavily on the personal rapport he has with Philemon. Multiple times Paul highlights his imprisoned state, their partnership for the gospel, and how much Onesimus means to him. He assumes that for the sake of their relationship, Philemon will in the end meet his appeal. In general, what is striking about Paul's ministry is that he was never too busy to invest in deep relationships. He probably intuited from Christ's own example that reconciliation and mediation presuppose relationships. Mediators will often enjoy deep relationships with both sides.

Second, instead of addressing the issue head-on, Paul invites Philemon to take a step back and consider broader categories. As we indicated already, he challenges Philemon to consider the well-being of others, in particular the believers who meet in his house. How will his refusal to love and receive Onesimus affect them? He also challenges Philemon to think in terms of eternity. Formerly, Onesimus was an earthly servant; but now, in Christ, he is a beloved brother who will be with Philemon forever. All this is because both have been saved by God's mercy. Indeed, eternity has an uncanny way of putting things in perspective. This is what Paul is asking Philemon to consider—to gain perspective as one destined with all the saints for eternal glory. Finally, he indirectly challenges Philemon to recall how his own debt was canceled by Christ's death on the cross. Whatever we owed to God because of our sin was paid for by the blood of Christ. This reality cannot but influence—if not dictate—how we engage those that have wronged us.

A good friend of mine, much older, much wiser, regularly says, "Most of the time, you have to help people arrive at things on their own. You can't just tell them what they're doing wrong or what they should do." This is what Paul is doing. To be sure, as an apostle he could have just ordered Philemon to do what was required. But he was not concerned primarily with compliance but more so with obedience from the heart. In the end, he knew that obligatory obedience leads to minimal obedience. For Philemon and Onesimus, it would have amounted to a formal and polite coexistence. Paul makes clear that this is not what he was looking for. As Philemon would have prepared a bed and made time for conversation with Paul, so now he must do the same—and more—for Onesimus. This sort of deep and lasting change is only possible through a repentant and renewed heart. Knowing that a direct approach would have likely evoked a defensive posture, Paul adopts a more personal, circuitous, but nevertheless effective route. In our efforts to facilitate peace, we would also benefit from thinking through not just the things we say but also how we say them. A relational, communal, theological—and indirect—approach will likely yield superior results even if it requires that much more patience and deliberation.

Finally, the Letter to Philemon underscores the necessity of accountability. Reconciliation simply doesn't come naturally. It's best if we're honest about this from the outset. My sphere of work includes pastors and seminary professors, men and women who are supposed to stand as pillars and propagators of the faith. But all will attest that reconciliation continues to be a major struggle. For reasons we have stated (and not stated), it's difficult to pick up the phone and ask to meet for coffee to reconcile. We prefer to pretend that all is well. This is why Paul concludes the letter by making clear to Philemon: "I plan to visit you as soon as I'm out of prison. And, by the way, all our mutual colleagues, who are well aware of the situation, send greetings." Nothing like a little pressure, the apostle reasons.

Accountability protects us from the dangerous pit of self-sufficiency. Even as we discern God's will by living in intimate community, so too we find supernatural grace to overcome sin through the ordinary means of fellowship with believers. In my own experience, communicating to a brother my plans to initiate and pursue reconciliation with this or that person has done wonders to getting it done—more so, dare I say, than even praying over the matter. Obviously, I'm not downplaying the significance of prayer, nor am I seeking to pit prayer and accountability against each other. Both are needed—that is exactly the point. Much prayer and much accountability. "God, grant me grace to do the thing you require," we will pray. God's answer—perhaps to our disappointment—will not come in the form of an extraordinary outpouring of his Spirit but through the gentle yet firm words of another Christian.

As we conclude, it is worth quoting Wright's summary:

> It is a letter which, at one level 'about' *koinōnia*, Christian fellowship and mutual participation, is at a far deeper level an outworking, in practice, of that principle. That which it expounds, it also exemplifies. It is a living fragment of the life of Christ, working itself out in the lives of human beings so different from us and yet so similar. Perhaps the only hermeneutical principle we need here is the crisp command, issued in another context where custom and faith were in collision: go, and do thou likewise.[3]

---

3. Wright, *Epistles*, 170.

Bibliography

Bonhoeffer, Dietrich. *Life Together: The Classic Exploration of Faith in Community.* Translated by John W. Doberstein. New York: Harper & Row, 1954.

Calvin, John. *Calvin's New Testament Commentaries: A Harmony of the Gospels: Matthew, Mark & Luke, Vol. 1.* Translated by A. W. Morrison. Edited by David W. Torrance and Thomas F. Torrance. Grand Rapids: Eerdmans, 1972.

Duhigg, Charles. *The Power of Habit: Why We Do What We Do In Life and Business.* New York: Random House, 2014.

Frame, John M. *Systematic Theology: An Introduction to Christian Belief.* Phillipsburg, NJ: P&R, 2013.

Jeon, Paul S. *Unreconciled: The New Norm.* Eugene, OR: Wipf & Stock, 2018.

Keller, Gary, with Jay Papasan. *The One Thing: The Surprisingly Simple Truth Behind Extraordinary Results.* London, UK: John Murray, 2013.

Lucas, Dick. *The Message of Colossians & Philemon.* The Bible Speaks Today. Downers Grove, IL: InterVarsity, 1980.

Moo, Douglas. *The Letters to the Colossians and to Philemon.* Grand Rapids: Eerdmans, 2008.

O'Brien, Peter. *Colossians, Philemon.* World Biblical Commentary 44. Waco, TX: Word, 1982.

Walls, Jeannette. *The Glass Castle: A Memoir.* New York: Scribner, 2005.

Wiersbe, Warren W. *The Bible Exposition Commentary: New Testament, Volume 1.* Colorado Springs, CO: Victor, 2001.

Wright, N. T. *The Epistles of Paul to the Colossians and to Philemon: An Introduction and Commentary.* The Tyndale New Testament Commentaries. Grand Rapids: Eerdmans, 1986.

www.ingramcontent.com/pod-product-compliance
Lightning Source LLC
LaVergne TN
LVHW051708080426
835511LV00017B/2802